THE ORIO]
LITTLE BOOK

Other "Little Books of Wisdom" Titles Available

THE ORIOLES FAN'S
LITTLE BOOK OF WISDOM

Bucky Fox

Taylor Trade Publishing
Lanham • New York • Boulder • Toronto • Plymouth, UK

Published by Taylor Trade Publishing
An imprint of The Rowman & Littlefield Publishing Group, Inc.
4501 Forbes Boulevard, Suite 200, Lanham, Maryland 20706
www.rlpgtrade.com

Estover Road, Plymouth PL6 7PY, United Kingdom

Distributed by NATIONAL BOOK NETWORK

Library of Congress Cataloging-in-Publication Data

Fox, Bucky.
  The Orioles fan's little book of wisdom / Bucky Fox.
    p. cm.
  ISBN-13: 978-1-58979-346-0 (pbk. : alk. paper)
  ISBN-10: 1-58979-346-3 (pbk. : alk. paper)
  1. Baltimore Orioles (Baseball team)—Miscellanea. 2. Baltimore Orioles (Baseball team)—History. I. Title.

GV875.B2F69 2008
796.357'64097526—dc22

2007039850

Grand Dedication

To women who touch all the bases:

First, Donna LeMon, a sister who proudly leads our family's lineup.

Second, Debbie King, a sister who comes through when it counts.

Third, Pam Bogdonoff, a sister still rooting for Brooks Robinson.

Fourth, Maria Fox, a wife who keeps me steady at home plate.

Introduction

How do you translate Baltimore Orioles fan?

It means:

- Loving that steal of Frank Robinson from Cincinnati just before his Triple Crown season of 1966.
- Going nuts while Brooks Robinson vacuumed those Reds in the 1970 World Series.
- Enjoying Rick Dempsey's clown act and World Series MVP show in 1983.
- High-fiving Cal Ripken for solidifying his Iron Man streak in 1995.
- Cheering Miguel Tejada for winning the All-Star Game's MVP Award in 2005.
- Reliving so much Orioles history through the Web sites Baseball-Reference .com (particularly Sean Forman), Baseball-Almanac.com, BaseballLibrary .com, BaseballHallofFame.org, SportsIllustrated.com, ESPN.com, MLB.com

(especially O's PR chief Bill Stetka), TheBaseballPage.com, Wikipedia.org, OCRegister.com, LATimes.com, Baltimore.org, MinorLeagueBaseball.com, BallParksofBaseball.com, BaltimoreSun.com, WashingtonPost.com, RobNeyer .com, Oobleck.com, and LatinoSportsLegends.com—plus *Get in the Game*, the 2007 book Ripken wrote with Donald Phillips.
- Trying to make this book as clean as a Brian Roberts double in 2007, thanks to the eagle eyes of my sister Debbie King, my buddies Tony Batt and Paul Whitfield, and editors Rick Rinehart, Jehanne Schweitzer, and Meghann French at Taylor Trade Publishing.
- Hoping the Orioles win another World Series.

Bucky Fox
October 2007

O, Say This Team Is Patriotic

The Baltimore Orioles go by another nickname that's as short as they come: O's. And do Orioles fans ever let everyone hear it. During the national anthem before every game, Baltimore's backers bellow, "O! say does that star-spangled banner yet wave."

You could say anthem author Francis Scott Key knew during the bombardment of Baltimore's Fort McHenry in 1814 that the O's would fly into town 140 years later.

It's Best to Be Frank

When considering the greatest Oriole of all, Frank Robinson could be at the top of the order. He simply turned Baltimore into the best team in baseball as soon as he donned the black and orange.

The year was 1966. The Orioles contended two years before, but hadn't won anything since shedding their St. Louis Browns colors and moving to Maryland in 1954. Now Robinson was on the team, and suddenly these Birds were flying high.

With Robinson crushing the ball for a .316 average, 49 home runs, and 122 runs batted in—leading the American League in all three groups for the Triple Crown—the O's soared to the pennant. No wonder he was voted the AL's Most Valuable Player.

He quickly led the Orioles to the world championship.

When You See a Title, Call It

Jon Miller, a husky man, bulked up his broadcasting résumé by calling *Sunday Night Baseball* for ESPN. By 2007 he was one of the biggest announcers in the game, also doing play-by-play for the Giants in his native San Francisco. But he was big way before that, building his national reputation as the voice of the Orioles from 1983 to 1996. He came into Baltimore a winner and left the same way, with the Orioles reaching the playoffs both of those years.

That 1983 debut was really special. As in World Series special. When the O's won it in Philadelphia, it was Miller time: "Everybody else is in muted silence. The pitch! Line drive! Ripken catches it at shortstop! And the Orioles are champions of the world!"

Numbers Can Make You Look Good

The Orioles retired numbers that make one strong team:

4: Earl Weaver, manager
22: Jim Palmer, pitcher
33: Eddie Murray, first baseman
5: Brooks Robinson, third baseman
8: Cal Ripken Jr., shortstop
20: Frank Robinson, outfielder

When Baltimore gets around to retiring a catcher, a second baseman, and two more outfielders, the numbers standing up by Oriole Park at Camden Yards could field a solid defense.

Taking Your Time Can Be Worth It

When the Birds won the World Series in 1966, they finally caught up with every other team in the original American League. Going back to 1901, the Junior Circuit looked like this: Chicago White Stockings, Boston Americans, Detroit Tigers, Philadelphia Athletics, Baltimore Orioles, Washington Senators, Cleveland Blues, and Milwaukee Brewers. Those Brewers were actually the forefathers of the modern-day Orioles. The Milwaukee franchise moved to St. Louis in 1902 and renamed itself the Browns. By 1954 they were playing in Baltimore as the O's.

As for that Baltimore team in 1901, it moved two years later to New York and eventually took on the name Yankees. So if you look at that 1901 AL, seven franchises had won world titles by 1935—and the Orioles made it eight in 1966.

Get a Kick Out of Managing

Earl Weaver stepped into the Hall of Fame because he kicked up a storm on the diamond. Literally. He stomped on the field, dusted up the plate, and yelled at umps so often, he was ousted 98 times. Through the 2007 season, that ranked number fourth all time, according to TheBaseball Page.com. Picture the Earl of Baltimore, and you see his cap turned backward and his face turning red in front of the men in blue. Listen to Weaver, and you hear this: "The job of arguing with the umpire belongs to the manager, because it won't hurt the team if he gets thrown out of the game."

If the Game Needs Repair, Break a Record

A year after the player strike zapped the 1994 World Series, Cal Ripken struck.

The whole season of 1995, the Baltimore shortstop never stopped. And when September 6 popped up, he stretched his streak to 2,131 straight games, breaking Lou Gehrig's great record. For the Iron Man's golden night, Oriole Park packed in 46,272 fans. One of them was President Bill Clinton, who celebrated in the radio booth with O's announcer Jon Miller when Ripken ripped a homer in the fourth inning on the way to Baltimore's 4-2 victory over the California Angels.

What's in a Number? Plenty

Baltimore fans will forever remember Cal Ripken Jr. for two numbers: 2,632 and 8. The bigger tally forever stamps Ripken the Iron Man, playing game after game from May 30, 1982, through September 19, 1998. The number 8 forever stays retired at Camden Yards.

From his 2007 book, *Get in the Game*: "So I began to think in depth about my streak. . . . I came up with eight elements, which I found somewhat ironic because the number I wore on my back for those 21 major league seasons was 8. . . . (1) the right values, (2) a strong will to succeed, (3) love what you do, (4) preparation, (5) anticipation, (6) trusting relationships, (7) life management, and (8) the courage of your convictions."

If You're Looking for the Pearl of Maryland, Check Out the Earl of Baltimore

Weaver reined in a pile of victories—1,480 in all against 1,060 losses for a .583 percentage during his Orioles reign from 1968 to 1982, and again in 1985 and '86. That last season was his only losing one. And as of 2007 his .583 winning percentage ranked seventh on the all-time list among managers lasting at least 10 years. Weaver simply won when it counted. He didn't care about spring training games. His line about his Florida days went like this: "No one's gonna give a damn in July if you lost a game in March."

Don't Just Be an Earl; Be a King

Earl Weaver oversaw the greatest run in Orioles history—and one of the top eras in baseball annals. Playing the Oriole Way, Weaver's men set the sport's standard. They finished lower than second place just twice from 1969 to '82. They were so dominant that they won at least 100 games five times. Want more? They set American League records with 217 victories over two seasons (1969–70) and 318 over three campaigns (1969–71).

Overall, Weaver Ball produced six Eastern Division titles, four American League pennants, and the World Series championship of 1970. The Missouri native showed 'em, all right. One Orioles general manager put it this way: "Earl built the machine and installed all the buttons!"

First Starts with F, as in Frank

The first player to win a Most Valuable Player trophy in both leagues? Frank Robinson. He collected the National League's while slugging for the Cincinnati Reds in 1961. He grabbed the American League's in his first season with the Orioles in 1966.

The first player to homer for both leagues in the All-Star Game? Frank Robinson. In 1959 at the Los Angeles Coliseum, he belted one against Chicago's Early Wynn in the NL's 5-3 losing effort. Then, in 1971 at Detroit's Tiger Stadium, he tagged Pittsburgh's Dock Ellis for a two-run shot to power the AL toward a 6-4 triumph.

The first Oriole to homer in a World Series? Frank Robinson. Back in LA, this time at Dodger Stadium, he gave the Birds a 2-0 lead in the very first inning of Game 1 of the 1966 Fall Classic.

Was Frank an Old 30? Bull

One of baseball's most unequal deals gave Baltimore the boost of all time.

It came before the 1966 season, with new personnel chief Harry Dalton making a brilliant trade: pitcher Milt Pappas and two other since-forgotten names to Cincinnati for a fellow named Frank Robinson. Result: instant dynasty for the Birds, wilderness years for the Reds.

In 2001 ESPN.com's Page 2 ranked the deal the seventh most lopsided trade in sports history. The site recalled Cincy general manager Bill De-Witt's infamous "old 30" label on F. Robby, who promptly produced his Triple Crown. The 1988 movie *Bull Durham* underscored the trade's lore with this Susan Sarandon line: "But bad trades are part of baseball. Now who can forget Frank Robinson for Milt Pappas, for God's sake?"

If One Slam Is Nice, Two Are Grand

Frank Robinson was born in Texas, so he knew about big: big homers—586 in all—and big runs batted in—a warlike 1,812 total. His birthplace was Beaumont, French for "beautiful mountain." He spent plenty of days in his Hall of Fame career looking good on the mountaintop—especially on June 26, 1970. While leading the Orioles toward their second world title, he swung a world-class bat, jacking back-to-back grand slams. His first bases-clearing homer came in the fifth inning. He came right back in the sixth for a replay, bringing the same runners—Dave McNally, Don Buford, and Paul Blair—home. The result was a 12-2 Baltimore triumph at Washington's RFK Stadium.

THE ORIOLES FAN'S LITTLE BOOK OF WISDOM •

We Are the World?
Well, Brooks Was

You could easily say the greatest performance in World Series history came from Baltimore's Brooks Robinson in 1970. He was so stellar with the glove and bat, he wore the Hickok Belt for that year's top athlete in all of sports. At third base, Brooks snatched every ball the Big Red Machine bashed his way, to the point that Johnny Bench lamented, "I will become a left-handed hitter to keep the ball away from that guy." Already a Human Vacuum Cleaner on defense, he turned into the Human Howitzer on offense, hitting .429 with two homers and six runs batted in during the Orioles' five-game triumph over Cincinnati.

15

Build Support, but Still Follow the Leader

The Orioles had plenty of heroes in the 1970 World Series as they avenged their upset loss to the Miracle Mets the previous year. Center fielder Paul Blair hit .474 to lead all Orioles. First baseman Boog Powell backed up his MVP season with two homers and five runs batted in. Lefty starter Dave McNally won Game 3 with his arm and bat, cracking a grand slam. Even so, it was Brooks Robinson at third base who had the Reds practically crying foul.

Pete Rose: "Brooks Robinson belongs in a higher league."
Sparky Anderson: "I hope the car they give him (as Series MVP) has an extra large glove box."

Better to Go with Two Robinsons

From 1966 to '71, the spark that gave Baltimore liftoff came from Robinson heat. With Frank and Brooks firing up the lineup, the Orioles rocketed to four pennants and two world titles. The right fielder and third baseman were called the Robinson Twins for a reason:

American League MVP: one each
World Series MVP: one each
All-Star MVP: one each
Hickok Belt: one each

No wonder Earl Weaver didn't worry about them: "I don't think, in all the years I managed them, I ever spoke more than 30 words to Frank and Brooks."

When Following the O's, You Might as Well Be Color-Blind

Frank and Brooks Robinson were so in tune, they harmonized for home runs in the first inning of the Birds' first World Series game in 1966. Did anyone see that Frank was black and Brooks was white? Or that Frank wore number 20 and Brooks wore number 5? Evidently it was tough to tell them apart, which explains their nicknames: F. Robby and B. Robby. Wondered F. Robby: "I don't see why you reporters keep confusing Brooks and me. Can't you see that we wear different numbers?"

18

When Judging, Get Your Numbers in Order

Frank Robinson led by banging the ball. Just look at his 586 homers. They ranked fourth all-time when he retired in 1976. He led by winning big. Check out his reaching five World Series—one with the Reds, four with the Orioles—and twice winning it all. He led by swinging big. Call up his postseason homers: 10.

Robinson also threw his weight around in the clubhouse. The Judge, as he was called, would lighten up the Orioles by donning a mop and running his Kangaroo Court. He would fine teammates for transgressions. Such as: Brooks Robinson, 1970 World Series star. His crime? Showboating.

19

Step to the Plate Softly and Carry a Big Stick

Frank Robinson carried such a big bat, he ranks as one of the top players in baseball history. Here's how top: In 1999 the Society for American Baseball Research polled its members and compiled a list of the 100 greatest of all time. Number 1 was Baltimore-born Babe Ruth, who played five months for the minor-league Orioles. Number 24 was Frank Robinson. Eight other Orioles joined the elite group: Brooks Robinson at number 32, Cal Ripken at 43, Jim Palmer at 57, Reggie Jackson at 67, Hoyt Wilhem at 77, Eddie Murray at 82, Robin Roberts at 83, and Luis Aparicio at 88. Three Browns made the list: George Sisler at 55, Eddie Plank at 94, and Rube Waddell at 97.

20

20 Is Really Just a Round Number

When Mike Mussina won his 246th game in August 2007, he passed another former Baltimore pitcher, Dennis Martinez, for an odd record. Both right-handers had been tied for the most career victories without a 20-win season. Mussina was pitching for the Yankees and long gone from Baltimore when he took over the all-time lead on that quirky list, but most of his victories came with the Orioles. Mussina, a native of Williamsport, Pennsylvania, joined the big leagues in 1991 and went on a tear for the O's, averaging a 17-8 record from 1992 to 1999. In all, he went 147-81 in his 10 years with the Birds, winning four Gold Gloves. By 2001 Mussina was striking it rich in New York. Martinez, a Nicaraguan, landed in Baltimore in 1976. In 1986 he left Baltimore for Montreal, where he pitched a perfect game in 1991. He retired in 1998 with a career record of 245-193.

Seeking the Best? Look Right Here

In their 2000 book *Baseball Dynasties*, Rob Neyer and Eddie Epstein nearly give the 1970 O's straight A's. Neyer rates them number 2 among all-time teams. Epstein places them third. In the "Baseball's Greatest Teams" section, BaseballLibrary.com points out: "The centerpiece of a dominant three-year run, the 1970 Baltimore Orioles are not so well remembered as the 1969 edition that was upset by the Miracle Mets or the 1971 club that featured four 20-game winners. While there was little difference between the three teams, the 1970 version staked its claim as the best of the bunch by accomplishing what the other two couldn't manage—winning the World Series." In a Replayer.com dream tournament, those 1970 O's ran all the way to the semifinals, losing to the 1998 New York Yankees, who went on to win it all.

Numbers and Names Can Add Up

How stout were those 1970 O's? Let's count the ways:

1. They rolled through the regular season at 108-54, one of the premier records in history.
2. They won the American League East by 15 games, then swept the Minnesota Twins 3-0 in the playoffs.
3. They made the Big Red Machine look like a clunker, wrecking Cincinnati 4-1 in the World Series.
4. They fielded the American League Most Valuable Player in first baseman Boog Powell; three Gold Glove winners in Davey Johnson, Brooks Robinson, and Paul Blair; three 20-game winners in Mike Cuellar, Dave McNally, and Jim Palmer; and seven All-Stars—those three pitchers, Powell, Johnson, and the two Robinsons.

23

Go with What's Right

Pitching marvel Jim Palmer had his right hand in Baltimore's three World Series titles, winning Game 2 in 1966, Game 1 in 1970, and Game 3 in 1983—making him the only pitcher in history to win Series games in three decades.

The best of all O's pitchers:

- Virtually clinched the '66 crown by beating Sandy Koufax and the Dodgers 6-0—becoming at 20 years old the youngest pitcher to complete a Series shutout.
- Won 20 games eight times and the Cy Young Award thrice.
- Never surrendered a grand slam in a 19-year all-Baltimore career that produced a 268-152 record and 2.86 ERA.

Look at Brooks Catch On

The greatest third baseman in baseball history? When it comes to glove alone, many fans grab one answer: Brooks Robinson. He was called the Human Vacuum Cleaner for a reason—he simply cleaned up nearly every ball hit his way. Proof? As of 2007 he held the American League record for career fielding percentage, .971, among third basemen. And how about this: He swept 16 straight Gold Glove Awards. No other player at the hot corner came close. Fans knew his prowess, which is why they gave him the most votes of any player on the All-Time Rawlings Gold Glove Team announced in 2007. Robinson, born in Little Rock, Arkansas, was a boulder in Baltimore. He played each of his innings with the O's—all 23 years—tied atop same-team tenure with Boston's Carl Yastrzemski.

That's Mister, Not Miss

Brooks Robinson simply didn't miss. He didn't miss many balls hit his way—or pitched at him. Known for his glove, Brooks also swung a mean bat, banging 2,848 hits and 268 homers. And he didn't miss many games. He joined the Orioles in 1955—their second season after moving from St. Louis—and played all the way to 1977, catching a ride on the Best Damn Team in Baseball. In his last two seasons, he yielded the bulk of third-base duties to Doug DeCinces. Cal Ripken, who played all 20 of his years in Baltimore, said in his book *Get in the Game* that he looked up to Mr. Oriole: "Brooks made me realize that, in my heart, I always wanted to be an Oriole."

You Want Big? Try Boog

Boog Powell looked like his nickname: 6 feet 4 inches, 240 pounds. As broadcaster Joe Garagiola said, "If he held out his arm, he'd be a railroad crossing." Swinging his lumber from the left side, Boog helped power the O's through their contending charge of 1964 to '74. His 37 homers and 121 runs batted in led the Birds to their 109 victories in 1969, and the first baseman took second in the MVP voting behind Minnesota's Harmon Killebrew. So the Floridian resurfaced in 1970. He swatted 35 homers with 114 runs batted in and this time won the MVP Award. Powell capped that 1970 title season by hitting .429 in Baltimore's playoff sweep of the Twins and jacking two homers in the World Series.

Streak to the Top

Cal Ripken's 2,632 straight games continued to have an iron grip on the sports world well after he broke Lou Gehrig's record in 1995. In 2001, ESPN readers ranked it number 2 among individual sports streaks behind Joe DiMaggio's 56-game hit mark of 1941. At the 2002 World Series, Ripken was honored for producing the Most Memorable Baseball Moment, topping Hank Aaron and his record-breaking homer of 1974. And in 2007 *USA Today* added to its 25th-birthday greatest-list series by naming the Oriole's streak number 2 among sports stories over the previous quarter century, right behind Boston's World Series triumph of 2004.

28

Cycle Out of a Rut

The Orioles in 2007 flapped their wings—not to mention bats and arms—with nary a rise. Their standing was so low, they fired manager Sam Perlozzo in June and handed bench coach Dave Trembley the job. While the O's staggered to their 10th straight losing season with a 69-93 record—including an embarrassing 30-3 loss—an Ohioan named Aubrey Huff cycled into history. With 36,000 fans at Oriole Park cheering for him on the night of June 29, the first baseman hit for the cycle—tripling in the second inning, doubling in the fourth, homering in the fifth, and singling in the seventh. He was the first Oriole to pull off the feat at home. The only other Orioles to hit for the cycle were Cal Ripken in 1984 and Brooks Robinson in 1960—both on the road. The Orioles lost the Huff game 9-7 to the Los Angeles Angels, but he ate it up: "As a 235-pound fat guy, you get a triple out of the way, that's something."

29

Sometimes Wee Means Big

During the Orioles' previous life—in the National League in the late 19th century—they played like giants behind Wee Willie Keeler. They won three straight pennants from 1894 to 1896, then Keeler streaked on his own. He hit in the first 44 games of 1897, a single-season record that held up until Joe DiMaggio's 56-gamer of 1941 and an NL mark that Pete Rose tied in 1978. Keeler finished that campaign with a .424 average on the way to a career .341 mark. In 1898 the Orioles' right fielder was at it again, this time swatting 206 singles, a record Seattle's Ichiro Suzuki broke in 2004. Keeler's .385 average led the NL for the second straight season. All that while playing at just 5 feet 4, 140 pounds. His plaque entered the Hall of Fame up the road in Cooperstown, New York, in 1939. His secret to his big success? "Hit 'em where they ain't."

30

When You're Streaking, Follow a Moose

Mike Mussina saved his best for 1995. Specifically, September 6. On the night Cal Ripken broke the consecutive-games record, Moose made sure the result was victorious. Mussina mowed down the California Angels, fanning seven in seven-plus innings. He got the W in the historic game, a 4-2 Baltimore victory at Camden Yards. By the time that season ended, the righty had a 19-9 record, his best as of 2007. He had also turned Ripken's hitting around. "I had actually come out of a slump after having a conversation with Mike Mussina," the Iron Man wrote in *Get in the Game*. "He'd noticed that I was a bit jumpy and encouraged me to focus on my crouch and flatten out my swing a little bit. From that point on, things just clicked for me."

For Something Nice, Name It Twice

The Orioles' ballpark opened in downtown Baltimore in 1992. So what to call it? Eli Jacobs, who owned the team from 1989 to 1993, liked Oriole Park. William Schaefer, governor of Maryland from 1987 to 1995, voted for Camden Yards. Solution: Use both names. So officially it goes by Oriole Park at Camden Yards. Fans usually call it by either moniker, but mostly Camden Yards. Why Camden? That's what people called the rail yards, built at the turn of the century, that once bustled at the site. Going further back, it came from Charles Pratt, Earl of Camden, who stood up for civil liberties in 18th-century England. This earl never stood at the plate, much less argued at it. Some Baltimoreans preferred to name the park after Babe Ruth, born a few blocks away in 1895. But he never played major-league ball in Baltimore. So Oriole Park at Camden Yards it is.

32

Open the Way for a Shutout

The first batter to step to the plate at Camden Yards was Cleveland's Kenny Lofton. The day was April 6, 1992, with 44,568 nearly filling the new park. Baltimore righty Rick Sutcliffe threw the first pitch and quickly got Lofton to fly to right. Joe Orsulak caught it for the stadium's very first out. Sutcliffe went the distance for a 2-0 Baltimore triumph. Both scores came in the fifth inning. Catcher Chris Hoiles doubled home DH Sam Horn for the historical first run in the fifth inning. Oriole Park became a huge hit. Capacity was 48,000-plus, and the O's drew an average of 43,000-plus the first decade in their new digs. The ballpark turned out to be as enlightening as its namesake Earl of Camden. As the first of the new throwback stadiums, it set the tone for 15 fields similar to it—from Cleveland's Jacobs Field, which opened in 1994, to the 2006 edition of Busch Stadium in St. Louis.

33

With the Right Manager, You'll Grow

Hank Bauer, whose surname means "farmer" in German, had Baltimore blooming as soon as he planted his cleats in Memorial Stadium's dirt. Dusting it up was nothing new for this native of East St. Louis, Illinois. He was battle-tested as a Marine in World War II. He was a Yankee in the World Series—swatting hits in a record 17 straight games in the Fall Classic from 1956 to '58. Getting his hands dirty as Orioles manager after grabbing the reins in 1964, he quickly had them in their first pennant race. They won 97 games to finish just behind his old Yankees. They came back for more in 1965, winning 94 games. Then came the Bauer boom. Just like in his Bronx Bomber days, he led the Orioles to the world championship in 1966.

If It's Bauer, Take Cover

Hank Bauer was such a national hero, he appeared on the cover of *Time* magazine in September 1964. Two years later, the rest of baseball took cover while this muscular manager lifted the Orioles and the World Series trophy. How tough was he? "His face looks like a closed fist," wrote Pulitzer Prize–winning columnist Jim Murray. How sharp was he? "On the plays Hank has pulled that I don't agree with, he has proved to be right 95% of the time," said Hall of Famer Brooks Robinson.

If You Win,
You Better Keep Winning

All Hank Bauer did was win. He played on seven World Series winners as a Yankees outfielder, and he managed the Orioles to their first world title. Yet that was soon old news. Bauer's Orioles slumped to 76-85 the next year. And even though he had the team over .500 at the All-Star break in 1968, the O's fired him, and General Manager Harry Dalton boosted his old farm favorite, Earl Weaver, from first base coach to manager. So Bauer of East St. Louis bowed to Weaver of St. Louis. But no Orioles fan can forget the Bauer of Baltimore.

"Just remember," he said, "if you ream me, I got the last ream."

One Day You're Leading; the Next You're Followed by Weaver

The Hank Bauer/Earl Weaver succession had a spin-off: the Joe Altobelli/ Earl Weaver story. There was Bauer winning the World Series of 1966, only to leave in mid-1968, despite a winning record, to make room for the author of Weaver Ball: pitching, defense, and the three-run homer. Then came Altobelli in 1983. All he did was win the World Series immediately, only to leave in mid-1985 despite a winning record. The clubhouse door again opened for Weaver.

(37)

Come Home Fast

Cal Ripken was hardly rip-roaring fast. That explains his mere 36 stolen bases through 21 seasons, topping out at six in 1991. And yet rookie Ripken pulled off his first steal by going the toughest of routes: toward home plate. It came on May 31, 1982, at Baltimore's Memorial Stadium. The Birds were tied 3-3 with the Texas Rangers in the sixth inning. As Ripken recounted in his book *Get in the Game*: "It was the front end of a double steal, with Lenn Sakata on first and Al Bumbry at the plate. We put on a trick play where Lenn faked a move to second at the same time I took off for home. When the left-handed pitcher, Jon Matlock, whose back was to me, stepped off the mound to throw to first, he suddenly realized that I was heading home. But it was too late. I slid in under the tag in what was a close play." The Orioles won 8-7.

If You're Going to Break Through, Go with Robinson

Starting in 1956, Frank Robinson played 21 seasons in the big leagues: 10 with the Reds, six with the Orioles, one with the Dodgers, two with the Angels, and two and change with the Indians. It was during that stint in Cleveland that he crashed the kind of barrier another Robinson—Jackie—had broken two decades before. When the Indians hired Frank as manager in 1975, he became baseball's first black skipper. The Tribe had a rare winning record under him in 1976—then gave him the ax the next season. He later managed the San Francisco Giants (1981–84) and the Montreal Expos/Washington Nationals (2002–06) and, failing to generate his old Orioles magic, never made the playoffs.

Just Like Frank, You Can Go Home Again

Frank Robinson thought he was home for good in 1988. That's when he took over the Orioles as manager. Talk about starting at the bottom. The Birds teetered at 0-6 when F. Robby entered the clubhouse. They kept diving into the abyss until they reached 0-21—the worst start in baseball history through 2007. By the time that 1988 misery ended, the O's were 54-107, light-years behind the division's next-worst team, his old Indians. Then came 1989. Robinson had the Birds in the AL East hunt instantly. They went 87-75, just two games out of first, and he won American League Manager of the Year honors.

40

You're Loyal to Dad, but That Doesn't Make You Blind

If ever a player could have rebelled at Baltimore's managing change of 1988, it was Cal Ripken Jr. The victim was his father. Cal Sr. followed Earl Weaver's weak comeback and managed the O's of 1987 to a 67-95 mark, 31 games out of first place. So when he got the Birds out of the gate at 0-6 the next season, the O's said bye-bye—and hello to Frank Robinson, who came down from management to wear the O's cap. How did Cal Jr. take it from his shortstop vantage? He put it this way in *Get in the Game*, two decades later: "In essence, I gave Frank the benefit of the doubt, and he did not let me down. Not only did he later help me out of a terrible batting slump, but he also brought back my father as his third base coach."

Play Second, Manage First

Davey Johnson turned the twin killing like no other Oriole. He starred at second base, and won as manager. The Floridian took his stand as Baltimore's second baseman from 1966 to '72. He was an American League All-Star three times and also nabbed the Gold Glove thrice. To make sure everyone would remember him, Johnson swatted the last hit against the Dodgers great Sandy Koufax in Game 2 of the 1966 World Series; made the last out of the 1969 Series, flying out to the Mets' Cleon Jones; and with the Atlanta Braves in 1973 set the record for homers by a second baseman, with 43. Ten years after managing the Mets to the 1986 World Series title, Johnson returned to Baltimore and soon won a division championship.

42

Turn Left for the Right Way

Dave McNally—just like Rand McNally—was all over the map during the Birds' hot road show. He braked—stopping the Dodgers 1-0 at Baltimore's Memorial Stadium to complete the Orioles' sweep of the 1966 World Series. He streaked—going 15-0 to start the 1969 season before losing 5-2 at Minnesota's Metropolitan Stadium. He steered—getting his lefty delivery past those Twins for 11 strikeouts and winning Game 2 of the 1969 playoffs 1-0 at Memorial. He swung—becoming the first pitcher to hit a World Series grand slam, beating the Reds 9-3 in Game 3 in Baltimore. He drove—shifting from a Game 5 start and loss at Pittsburgh's Three Rivers Stadium to win Game 6 in relief at Memorial during the 1971 World Series. He parked—stopping in his hometown of Billings, Montana, after a 14-year career with 184 victories.

The Real World Series

When the World Baseball Classic swung open for business in 2006, the Orioles stepped up big time. The O's fielded 11 players to lead all big-league teams. Shortstop Miguel Tejada and pitcher Daniel Cabrera played for the Dominican Republic. Catcher Javy López and outfielder Luis Matos played for Puerto Rico. Erik Bedard and Adam Loewen pitched for Canada. Pitcher Rodrigo López and catcher Geronimo Gil played for Mexico. Bruce Chen pitched for Panama. Ramón Hernández caught for Venezuela. And John Stephens pitched for Australia. Japan won the tournament by beating Cuba 10-6 in the final at San Diego's Petco Park.

Keep Catching On

Many Baltimore fans honor Brooks Robinson with the tag "Mr. Oriole." Some give it to Cal Ripken Jr. And then there's Ellie Hendricks. Ripken is one of his endorsers. In his book *Get in the Game*, Ripken lauds the catcher as "one of the finest humanitarians who ever lived in the Baltimore, Maryland, area. In many ways, he truly was Mr. Oriole. After spending a team-record 37 years with our club, Elrod died suddenly of a heart attack in 2005. He was a wonderful man. No one could have done more." Before running Baltimore's bull pen for three decades, Hendricks played the bulk of his career as the Birds' lefty-hitting catcher. Platooning with Andy Etchebarren, Hendricks was a cog in the pitching-powered pennant winners of 1969 to '71.

45

Come Through When It Counts

Ellie Hendricks was born in the Virgin Islands. By the time he landed in Baltimore at age 27 in 1968, he made sure to stick. His platooning stick averaged 10 homers a year his first four seasons. He finished his career with 62 homers and only a .220 average, but he positively caught the moment in three postseason series. In the 1969 American League Championship Series, Hendricks' two doubles plated three to help Baltimore bomb Minnesota 11-2 in Game 3's clincher. In the 1970 World Series opener, his game-tying homer in the fifth inning and his play against Cincy's Bernie Carbo at the plate in the sixth inning sparked the O's to a 4-3 victory. Hendricks went on to hit .364 in Baltimore's five-game triumph. The next year, Hendricks was at it again. His homer off Catfish Hunter helped Baltimore beat Oakland 5-1 in Game 2 of the ALCS, which the Orioles completed the next day.

A Road Trip Can Lead to Cuba

The Orioles threw a curve in 1999: They went to Cuba to play baseball. This was the same Cuba that America quit dealing with after Fidel Castro traded his pitching glove for his dictator's iron fist—punctuated by the Cuban missile crisis of 1962. Nearly four decades after presidents Dwight Eisenhower and John Kennedy told Castro to stuff his cigars, the Orioles warmed up to the idea of hopping down from their Florida training camp and trying to light up Cuban pitching. So on March 28, 1999, the Birds played the Cuban national team in Havana, and the visitors won 3-2. Harold Baines provided the difference by singling home Will Clark in the 11th inning. The game marked the first time a major-league team hit Cuba since the Los Angeles Dodgers and Cincinnati Reds played an exhibition series there in 1959.

47

If You Like It, Play Two

The 1999 Orioles-Cuba game in Havana packed Latinoamericano Stadium to the tune of 50,000. Cuban boss Fidel Castro shook hands with Baltimore players, then sat with O's owner Peter Angelos and Baseball Commissioner Bud Selig to watch the Birds' triumph. The Orioles liked it so much, they returned the invitation. So on May 3, 1999, the Cuban all-stars landed at 48,000-strong Camden Yards and hardly played like polite visitors. They doubled the Birds 12-6. Harold Baines again gave Baltimore the lead, this time with a double in the first inning, but Cuba quickly began to look like the Olympic champion of three years before.

48

Shortstop Can Be Anything But

When it comes to shortstops, the Orioles keep going. Recent fans know the power of Cal Ripken and Miguel Tejada. Baltimore backers with longer memories recall two others short on slugging and long on fielding: Luis Aparicio and Mark Belanger. Aparicio came from Venezuela, first starring with the Chicago White Sox and then joining the Orioles in 1963. He won two of his Gold Gloves while in Baltimore and helped the O's to the 1966 world title. When Aparicio left two years later, Belanger stuck his glove in there. Like his old roommate, the Blade didn't handle a Silver Bat, just Gold Gloves—eight from 1969 to '78. And like the South American, the native of Pittsfield, Massachusetts, was money in a World Series run, this one in 1970. He was fortunate to be a part of double-play Gold Gloves— with Davey Johnson in 1971 and with Bobby Grich from 1973 to '76.

49

Make the Outfield the In Crowd

The Orioles owned the American League from 1969 to '71 because of pitching, homers, defense—and a mighty outfield. Frank Robinson said it all in right, then came Paul "Motormouth" Blair in center and understated Don Buford in left. Blair, an Oklahoman, simply defined the "out" in outfield. He grabbed eight Gold Gloves from 1967 to '75, and in the 1966 World Series, his stab of Jim Lefebvre's shot in the eighth inning of Game 4 just about clinched Baltimore's 1-0 victory. That came a day after Blair's homer in Game 3 was all the O's needed in a 1-0 triumph. Buford, a Texan, won no Gold Gloves, but was a swift and clutch leadoff man. He led the league in runs, with 99 in 1971, and had a .472 on-base percentage in three straight ALCS sweeps. Wrote baseball researcher Bill James, "Don Buford was one of the really underrated players in baseball history."

Swing Left, Swing Right, Swing Hard

Eddie Murray grew up in Los Angeles, and he played there for both baseball teams, the Dodgers and Angels. In 2006 he was 50 and back on the West Coast for a short stint as the Dodgers' hitting coach. Tucked in that sunshine of a baseball career, Murray displayed his most muscle in a city far from the palm trees: Baltimore. He liked the East Coast so much that he played for the O's twice—from 1977 to '88, then for the second half of 1996. Not just played, but starred: In the 13 years he switch-hit for the Orioles, Murray turned into probably the greatest first baseman in their history.

When You Want to Show Off Your Biggest Number, Go Home and Do It

Eddie Murray, who played for six teams, saved his most historic blast for Baltimore. It came on September 6, 1996, at Oriole Park with nearly 47,000 fans urging him to park his 500th homer. Steady Eddie obliged in the seventh inning: With Detroit righty Felipe Lira on the mound, Murray swung from the left side and jacked the ball over the center-field wall. The Orioles lost 5-4, but they were still playoff bound. And Murray whipped off a .400 batting average in their first-round triumph over Cleveland.

When You See Superstars, Shine Along with Them

Eddie Murray finished his playing days in 1997 in Los Angeles. His career numbers were hardy: 504 homers and 3,255 hits. How hardy were they? Well, figure that when he retired, only two other players stood in the 500/3,000 batter's box: Hank Aaron and Willie Mays, two of the greatest players in history. In 2005 a fourth player joined the club, and he happened to be another player who had his biggest moments with the Orioles: Rafael Palmeiro. The Cuban native amassed 3,020 hits and 569 homers in a 20-year career.

53

It Helps to Be a Hit

Of his two decades in the majors, Rafael Palmeiro played seven seasons with the Orioles. And he made sure to produce big time. In 1996 he led Baltimore to the playoffs by amassing 39 homers and 142 runs batted in. The next season his 38 jacks and 110 runs batted in helped lift the Orioles to the Eastern Division title. As of 2007, that 1997 team was Baltimore's last ticket to the playoffs. Palmeiro tried to drive the O's further. He blasted two homers in the 1996 American League Championship Series, which the Yankees won in five games. He hit another homer in the 1997 ALCS, which Cleveland won in six. The big first baseman/designated hitter went on to help the Texas Rangers reach the playoffs in 1999, then returned to Baltimore to finish his career in 2004 and '05.

When a Big Bat Breaks, So Can a Team

Eddie Murray swung into the 1979 World Series with one burly bat. He was fresh off a .417, five-RBI batting performance in the Orioles' playoff triumph over the California Angels. So it was no surprise when he started out crushing the ball in the Fall Classic, going four for five with a homer in the first two games. Then he hit nothing: Oh for 21. He wasn't alone. About the only Orioles who didn't vanish with him were shortstop Kiko Garcia, who finished at .400, and right fielder Ken Singleton, who hit .357. Still, Murray's meltdown was most dramatic, and the O's blew a 3-1 Series lead to the Pittsburgh Pirates. He had to live with that embarrassment the next three seasons.

It Helps to Speak Softly and Carry a Big Stick

For Eddie Murray, redemption came with the 1983 World Series. Again the Orioles led three games to one on the road in Pennsylvania. This time they were in Philadelphia, and Murray seized the moment. He homered in the second for a 1-0 Baltimore lead. Two innings later he blasted a two-run shot for a 4-0 O's lead. The Orioles went on to win the game 5-0 and the Series 4-1. Murray, so soft-spoken in public, had let his bat do some serious talking when it counted. Suddenly Murray was a money player, after going broke just four years before. It all paid off. His World Series bat landed in the Hall of Fame Museum in Cooperstown, New York, and he was inducted in 2003.

At First, Succeed

Six Orioles won Rookie of the Year trophies: Ron Hansen in 1960, Curt Blefary in 1965, Al Bumbry in 1973, Eddie Murray in 1977, Cal Ripken in 1982, and Gregg Olson in 1989. As far as franchise history goes, add Roy Sievers to the list. The outfielder, playing for his hometown St. Louis Browns, won the first American League rookie honor in 1949. Hansen displayed such power at shortstop, he made the All-Star team his first season. The Nebraskan finished with 22 homers and 86 runs batted in to help Baltimore go 89-65 for a stunning second-place finish in 1960. Blefary, a Brooklyn-born outfielder, also hammered 22 homers his first season. He came through with 70 runs batted in for a Baltimore team on the verge. The 1965 Birds went 94-68 and were one year away from winning it all.

Some Men Fight for Their Award

Al Bumbry was simply a quick hit on the way to collecting his Rookie of the Year trophy. Playing the outfield and a little designated hitter, he swatted .337, had a league-leading 11 triples, and stole 23 bases to help the Orioles to the 1973 American League East title. Bumbry was a Vietnam War Bronze Star hero from nearby Fredericksburg, Virginia, and had staying power. He produced 205 hits and stole 44 bases in the Birds' near miss of 1980 and finished with 254 steals in his 14-year career. Earl Weaver wasn't exactly a lover of stolen bases, but he liked drawing on Bumbry's speed. "I saved up enough one time [from cigarette coupons]," the manager told the *Sporting News*, "and got Al Bumbry."

Be a Hit from the Start

Eddie Murray was everywhere during his Rookie of the Year campaign of 1977. The future Gold Glove first baseman played 42 games at the position, plus three games in the outfield and 111 games at designated hitter. It didn't matter where he played. The man simply hit: 27 homers, 88 runs batted in, .283 average. Thanks to Murray, Baltimore went a surprising 97-64 to finish second in the AL East, just behind the eventual world champion New York Yankees. By the time he sat down after 20 years in the bigs, Murray would be the first switch-hitter to combine 500 homers with 3,000 hits.

59

A Switch Can Mean a Long Stop

Earl Weaver knew he had someone special as soon as Cal Ripken Jr. joined the Orioles organization. Maybe even before, since the son of the Birds' longtime minor-league manager grew up in nearby Aberdeen, Maryland. By the time Cal Jr. threw on a Baltimore uniform in August 1981, Weaver was sure. "There was nothing to keep him from being a star in the major leagues. That was inevitable," the manager said years later. Ripken played a little third base that season, but not enough to rate as a real rookie. The next season, Weaver made the tough call: He moved him to shortstop, where Ripken would produce a Hall of Fame career. The big newcomer came on like a banshee. He finished with 28 homers and 93 runs batted in to clinch the 1982 Rookie of the Year Award. Sophomore jinx? Forget it. The next season he won the first of his two Most Valuable Player Awards.

60

Welcome the All-Stars In

When the All-Star Game swings smack in the middle of the baseball season, TV viewers tune in to catch the game's great players. But fans have another option: Go to the Midsummer Classic. Orioles devotees had a chance to watch in their own town twice. In 1958 Memorial Stadium showcased the American League's 4-3 victory as almost 49,000 watched. Vice President Richard Nixon tossed the first pitch, and Baltimore lefty Billy O'Dell clinched it with three shutout innings for the save. The Orioles' other All-Star, Gus Triandos, started at catcher and singled in two at bats. In 1993 Oriole Park featured the AL's 9-3 rout of the Nationals, with 48,000 on hand. Cal Ripken started at shortstop, but went hitless in three at bats. Mike Mussina, amid a 14-6 season for the O's, warmed up in the ninth, but manager Cito Gatson didn't call for the righty—and the fans let him have it.

61

Looking for Stars?
Meet Them in St. Louis

The Orioles franchise actually played host to an early All-Star Game—in 1948, when the team was still the St. Louis Browns. And when the 15th version of the Midsummer Classic swung through Sportsman's Park, it made the American League feel right at home. The Junior Circuit won 5-2. With 34,000 watching, one local star appeared in American League garb: Al Zarilla, who played right field and went zip for two. The Los Angeles native would finish the season for the Browns hitting .329, fourth best in the AL.

If You Want the Most, Turn to the O's

What team has the most Most Valuable Player Awards in All-Star Game history? Baltimore. The Orioles grabbed the honor six times: Brooks Robinson in 1966, Frank Robinson in 1971, Cal Ripken in 1991 and 2001, Roberto Alomar in 1998, and Miguel Tejada in 2005. Through the 2007 Midsummer Classic, two teams stood right behind with five trophies each: the San Francisco Giants and Cincinnati Reds.

If You Want to Hit It Big, Do It in the All-Star Game

How did Baltimore players dominate the All-Star Game's MVP Award? By tagging the ball. Brooks Robinson won the trophy in a losing cause in 1966. He stung a triple off Sandy Koufax in a three-for-four day, but the National League won 2-1 in the 10th inning at St. Louis's Busch Stadium. In 1971, Frank Robinson crushed a two-run homer in the third inning to put the American League up for good at Detroit's Tiger Stadium. The result was a 6-4 triumph for the Earl Weaver–managed AL and stopped the Junior Circuit's eight-game losing streak.

In All-Star Settings, Let 'er Rip

As of 2007 Cal Ripken was the only American Leaguer to capture the All-Star Game's MVP Award twice. He power-grabbed it in 1991, when his three-run homer led the AL to a 4-2 victory at Toronto's Skydome. It was hardly shocking: Ripken pounded out his best homer and RBI numbers—34 and 114—on the way to the regular season's MVP trophy.

Ten years later Cal Jr. led the Junior Circuit again. This time he woke up Seattle. Having announced that this would be his last season, the Iron Man entered the batter's box in the third inning to a Safeco Field–shaking ovation. He responded by bashing the first pitch over the left-field wall. The AL won 4-1, and he won the All-Star MVP Award again.

65

O, Midsummer Can Be Fun

O's fans love bouncing to John Denver's "Thank God I'm a Country Boy." So it made sense that the Orioles struck the right chord at the singer's namesake town. The scene was Denver's Coors Field. The setting was the 1998 All-Star Game. The stars were Orioles: Roberto Alomar, Rafael Palmeiro, and Cal Ripken. Alomar shone brightest. The Puerto Rican second baseman—amid a 12-year run making the All-Star team and collecting 10 Gold Gloves—was solid in the field, and he bashed the ball in the mile-high air. His homer, stolen base, and three-for-four night landed him the game's MVP Award—a year after his brother Sandy won it. First baseman Palmeiro went two for two with an RBI. And Ripken, starting for the 15th straight time to break Willie Mays's record, doubled to drive in two runs. It added up to a 13-8 romp for the American League.

It's Fun to Join the In-Crowd

Baltimore's stamp on the All-Star Game MVP Award came mostly from infielders: third baseman Brooks Robinson in 1966, shortstop Cal Ripken in 1991 and 2001, Roberto Alomar in 1998 . . . and shortstop Miguel Tejada in 2005. Tejada, the Dominican who had landed in Baltimore the year before, opened the scoring with a homer in the second inning. He drove in a second run on a groundout, sparking the American League's 7-5 victory. Two other Baltimore infielders played. Second baseman Brian Roberts doubled and scored, and third baseman Melvin Mora struck out in his sole at bat. Orioles lefty B. J. Ryan pitched in the ninth inning and yielded a run, but the AL fans in Detroit's Comerica Park went home happy.

Play It Wild and Straight

The Orioles responded to Davey Johnson's leadership by clobbering a major-league record 257 homers and nailing down the 1996 AL wild-card spot. In their first postseason appearance in 13 years, the Orioles upset the Cleveland Indians in round one, then lost the pennant in five games to the New York Yankees. The next year Johnson won AL Manager of the Year honors while sparking his O's past the Yankees for the AL East title. The Orioles handled Seattle in the Division Series, then lost in six games to Cleveland. Johnson's Baltimore run was over. He handed in his uniform right after being named AL Manager of the Year, spent one season out of baseball, and then, in 1999, took over the team his Orioles had beaten three decades before in the World Series: the Los Angeles Dodgers.

68

Move In, Then Move Up

The Orioles took a while to shed their St. Louis Brownout. Upon landing in Baltimore in 1954, the team with the new colors looked the same. The O's went 54-100 that first season at Memorial Stadium, the same record they'd had the year before, when Sportsman's Park was their home. They played .438 baseball for the decade, barely getting off the ground in Maryland.

Then came a Baltimore revolution. It was called the 1960s. With Chuck Estrada leading a strong staff with an 18-11 mark, the 1960 O's shot into second place at 89-65, the franchise's first winning record since the end of World War II. The 1961 O's, behind Jim Gentile's rough 46 homers and 141 runs batted in, went 96-67.

Then came 1964, the Year of the Brooks.

69

If You Want Value, Turn to Third

Brooks Robinson turned the Orioles into true contenders in 1964. Thanks to his MVP production—.317 average, 28 homers, and 118 runs batted in—Baltimore battled for the pennant. The Orioles topped the American League by four and a half games on June 29 and still led by one game on September 15. The O's won seven of their last eight to finish at 97-65, but couldn't overcome the dynastic New York Yankees. Brooks had help. Boog Powell, a left fielder on those '64 O's, bashed 39 homers. Wally Bunker went 19-5 to lead the staff. And Lou Piniella appeared in four games, going zero for one—five years before he won the Rookie of the Year Award in Kansas City.

If You Want Power, Switch It On

Eddie Murray wasted little time blasting his way into Baltimore lore. After capturing Rookie of the Year honors in 1977, he made the American League All-Star team in 1978, the first of his eight appearances. He shared the American League home run title when he hit 22 in the strike-shortened 1981 season. When he retired after the 1997 season, his 1,917 runs batted in ranked first, his 504 homers second among switch-hitters. And as of 2007, his 19 grand slams stood third behind Lou Gehrig's 23 and Manny Ramirez's 20.

Sometimes the Bucs Stop You Here

The 1971 Orioles looked like they could have changed their name to Dynasty. They won 100 games for the third straight season, this time with a 101-57 record. They romped to the AL East title for the third straight year, this time by 12 games. They swept the AL pennant series a third straight time, this time drubbing Oakland. They were loaded with six All-Stars: Don Buford, Boog Powell, the Robinson boys, Mike Cuellar, and Jim Palmer. Their staff was armed with four 20-game winners. By the time the O's won Game 2 of the World Series 11-3 against Pittsburgh, they had fired off 16 wins in a row. This team was smokin'. And yet the Orioles fell one run short. They lost the seventh game of the World Series 2-1 to the Bucs. And so a Baltimore bunch that dominated baseball in so many ways from 1969 to '71 had just one world title to show for it.

For Sure, Go with Four

Those O's of 1971 featured four 20-game winners. How rare is that? The previous team to pull the feat played half a century before—the 1920 Chicago White Sox. Leading the way for those AL champion O's was Dave McNally. He went 21-5 with a 2.89 earned run average. Fellow lefty Mike Cuellar went 20-9 with an ERA of 3.08, high among the quartet. Pat Dobson came through by going 20-8 with a 2.90 ERA. It was by far the best production for this right-hander, a native of Buffalo, New York, whose career record was 122-129. Future Hall of Famer Jim Palmer solidified history by winning his 20th game on September 26 in Cleveland, beating the Indians 5-0. That gave him a 20-9 record along with an ERA of 2.68, the best on the starting staff. Besides going 81-31, the four arms completed 70 games.

Win Big with Big-Time Players

Entering the 2007 season, the Orioles owned three world championships. The team pulled off that triple play with plenty of stars, but mostly with this trio: the Robinsons and Rick Dempsey. Each was a World Series MVP. Frank Robinson came through in the 1966 Series with two homers, the second of which won the fourth game 1-0 to clinch the sweep. Brooks Robinson dominated the 1970 Series at third base and the plate, hitting .429 with two homers. Dempsey was clutch in the 1983 Series, swatting .385 and homering in the Game 5 clincher.

Catch Your Chance

Rick Dempsey took a call from Ronald Reagan on October 16, 1983, the night the catcher led the Orioles past the Phillies for baseball's championship. The president wanted to congratulate the country's latest hero. No doubt Dempsey got a kick out of chatting with the leader of the Free World. You can bet Reagan felt the same way while bantering with the leader of the World Series. The talk had to be fun. Reagan was about the funniest of presidents. Dempsey had his own routine, sliding all over the tarp during rain delays. On clear days, Dempsey was all business. He did a serious number for the Orioles in the 1983 Series, even twice gunning down the Phillies' speedy Joe Morgan. Then, as a backup catcher, he helped the Los Angeles Dodgers win it all in 1988.

75

Handle It Like Jack Dempsey

Rick Dempsey didn't punch like his namesake heavyweight boxing champion of the 1920s, but he sure hit and caught in superior fashion. Rick rose from Fayetteville, Tennessee, to become one of the greatest catchers in Baltimore history. After seven seasons with the Minnesota Twins and New York Yankees, he joined the Orioles in the middle of 1976. The next 10 years he helped the O's win two pennants—and a world title. Besides showing World Series sparks in 1983, he batted .400 in the 1979 American League pennant series as the O's handled the California Angels three games to one. Dempsey left Baltimore for Cleveland in 1987, then joined the Dodgers in 1988, the Brewers in 1991 and returned to the O's for a brief stay in 1992. After coaching for Baltimore through 2006, he had been in the majors five decades. Even the Manassa Mauler didn't have that kind of staying power.

Sometimes You Have One Shot

Reggie Jackson looked like a winner on the cover of *Sports Illustrated* in August 1976. He wore an O's uniform behind the headline "Hitting a Million." The right fielder would finish with 27 homers, helping Baltimore to second place. After that season, the Yankees spirited him off to New York with their millions of dollars. When he retired in 1987, he owned 563 homers, one of the grand totals in history. He never forgot Baltimore's spirit in '76, which he called one of his happiest. He certainly respected Earl Weaver, saying, "He is also one of the few baseball geniuses I have ever met."

Belt 'em Out,
Then Hope for a Belt

The most prestigious prize in sports over the third quarter of the 20th century was the Hickok Professional Athlete of the Year Award. It was commonly known as the Hickok Belt, derived from the belt-making Hickok Manufacturing Company in Rochester, New York. Every year, the firm gave an alligator-skin belt and gem-sparkling buckle to the top professional sportsman. The tradition lasted from 1950 to 1976, and in two of those years, Orioles won it. First came Frank Robinson in 1966, capping an amazing year: Triple Crown, regular-season MVP, and World Series MVP. Then came Brooks Robinson in 1970 for his superior World Series.

78

Hit and Throw Hard

Davey Johnson's Orioles won in 1996 and '97 with his Earl Weaver stand-bys: homers and pitching. The 1996 Birds claimed the wild card by bashing 257 homers—50 off the bat of center fielder Brady Anderson, who still held the team record heading into the 2008 season. That team total didn't last long as the major-league record, with the Seattle Mariners cracking 264 in 1997. On Baltimore's pitching side, Mike Mussina went 19-11. The fans loved it, flocking to Camden Yards to the tune of 3.6 million, tops in the American League. The 1997 Orioles did even better in the standings, taking the AL East crown—and at the turnstiles, with a league-best and team-record 3.7 million filling Oriole Park. Jeffrey Hammonds sparked the power with 21 homers in just 397 at bats. Reliever Randy Myers broke the team mark with 45 saves.

79

Lead with Your Left

Mike Flanagan came from New Hampshire. He liked that "New" better than its big brother: "I could never play in New York. The first time I ever came into a game there, I got in the bull pen car and they told me to lock the doors." Flanagan had fun with that line in 1979, when he and the Orioles beat up on New York's Yankees and the rest of the American League. The lefty flew to a 23-9 record with a league-high five shutouts and landed the Cy Young Award, while the Orioles—with Ken Singleton thrashing 35 homers—soared to a 102-57 record and the AL East title. He was the winning pitcher in Baltimore's 9-8 victory over the California Angels in Game 2 of the ALCS. In the World Series, he beat Pittsburgh 5-4 in Game 1. Flanagan still had enough to contribute to Oriole Magic in 1983, beating the Chicago White Sox 11-1 in Game 3 of the pennant series.

80

Try Stone for a Solid Season

Steve Stone threw everything he had into the 1980 season. He went 25-7 to win the Cy Young Award—the sixth time an Oriole won it in 11 years and the last time a Baltimore pitcher captured it as of 2007. The O's rode that right arm to a 100-62 record, three games behind the New York Yankees. On offense, those O's featured a 205-hit performance from center fielder Al Bumbry, plus surprising power from Benny Ayala, Dan Graham, Terry Crowley, and Gary Roenicke. Stone led a staff that included two previous Cy Young winners—Mike Flanagan and Jim Palmer—plus Scott McGregor, who went 20-8. Stone, hailing from Ohio, had never come close to winning 20 games in nine seasons. Now he owned the most wins in the majors. But the party was soon over. He went 4-7 in 1981, then left the game with arm trouble.

81

100 Isn't Always the Answer

When the Orioles missed the playoffs in 1980, they joined a rare group: teams since the World Series was canceled in 1904 that won 100 games and failed to reach the postseason. Entering the 2008 season, just seven other clubs had suffered that disappointment:

1909 Chicago Cubs
1915 Detroit Tigers
1942 Brooklyn Dodgers
1954 New York Yankees
1961 Detroit Tigers
1962 Los Angeles Dodgers
1993 San Francisco Giants

Hail the Halls

The National Baseball Hall of Fame Museum is a grand slam. It showcases Orioles such as Frank Robinson, it has videos of great baseball moments, it has souvenirs of everything from books to caps—and it's in the grandest of settings—Cooperstown, New York, with its pastoral beauty. The Hall of Fame is simply a huge hit, which is why ESPN in 2007 ranked it number 1 among baseball museums. The Orioles' own museum wasn't far behind: ESPN gave the Sports Legends Museum at Camden Yards its number 5 spot. ESPN.com lauded the shrine for offering "exhibits related to the two incarnations of the Baltimore Orioles (minor league and major league), to local sons like Babe Ruth and Cal Ripken Jr. and to the two Negro Leagues teams that once played in Baltimore."

83

Landrum and a Big Bang

Tito Landrum landed in Baltimore from St. Louis at midseason in 1983 and returned to the Gateway to the West the next year. In that short stint with the Orioles, the native of Joplin, Missouri, made a serious dent in Baltimore lore. Landrum's shot came in Game 4 of the American League pennant series. The Orioles led the Chicago White Sox two games to one. A victory would vault the O's from the best-of-five set into the World Series. If the Orioles lost, they would face a deciding game against LaMarr Hoyt, that year's Cy Young winner. With 45,000 roaring at Comiskey Park, the teams failed to score through nine innings. In the top of the 10th, righty-swinging Landrum stepped up with one out against lefty Britt Burns, still in after a long night of shutout pitching. Bang. The right fielder's homer shot the O's ahead 1-0. They went on to win 3-0 for the flag on the way to winning it all.

84

Lift That Stein to the Championship

One of John Lowenstein's lines went like this: "Nuclear war would render all baseball statistics meaningless." Lowenstein could afford to joke, because he was a lion and a rock—which his name reflects in German—at crunch time for the Orioles.

Baltimore faced desperation in the 1983 World Series when Lowenstein led off the fifth inning of Game 2 at Memorial Stadium. The home team trailed 1-0 in the Series and 1-0 on the scoreboard. Lowenstein responded by roaring—jacking a homer to tie the game—and the Birds flew to a 4-1 victory. They also soared to a 4-1 Series triumph.

Lowenstein hit .385 against Philadelphia. Together with his 1979 Fall Classic performance against Pittsburgh, his career World Series average was .308.

Have Fun Playing

ESPN's Chris Berman, who poured out nicknames, lifted one to the Orioles' left fielder in the 1980s: John "Tonight Let It Be" Lowenstein. The lefty swinger from Montana had his own fun lines:

"I flush the john between innings to keep my wrists strong."

"Sure, I screwed up that sacrifice bunt. But look at it this way: I'm a better bunter than a billion Chinese. Those suckers can't bunt at all."

"The secret to keeping winning streaks going is to maximize the victories while at the same time minimizing the defeats."

"If you act like you know what you're doing, you can do anything you want—except neurosurgery."

Play Baseball with Flying Colors

When the St. Louis Browns moved to Baltimore after the 1953 season, they shed the color of their nickname—and traded it for black and orange. Why those colors? They're the hues of the Maryland state bird. And so the reborn American League team took on the look and name of the Baltimore Orioles. Right away, the team cap boasted a silhouette Oriole. In 1966, as if anticipating their world crown, they jazzed up their caps with a cartoon Oriole face. By the late 1980s the Orioles frowned on that comic figure. A 0-21 start—like the one they suffered in 1988—can wipe a smirk off any Bird's face. So the next season they dug out that old full Oriole on black caps. They felt as if their wings were back, and indeed in 1989 they were.

When You're Great, Head for the Hall

Cal Ripken Jr. had to feel like a player again when he entered the National Baseball Hall of Fame on July 29, 2007. The crowd that day shook Cooperstown, New York, like a Baltimore playoff game, not an induction ceremony. Ripken sparked the excitement by being the 11th modern Oriole to join the Hall. The procession started with Robin Roberts in 1976. Then came Frank Robinson in 1982, Brooks Robinson and George Kell in 1983, Luis Aparicio in 1984, Hoyt Wilhelm in 1985, Jim Palmer in 1990, Reggie Jackson in 1993, Earl Weaver in 1996, and Eddie Murray in 2003.

The Best Can Make
It from Call to Hall

Ernie Harwell did the Orioles' play-by-play from 1954 to '59 before spending a marathon career in Detroit. Herb Carneal took the Orioles' ball through 1961 before making his airwave pitches in Minnesota. Then Chuck Thompson—mostly with Bill O'Donnell—called the greatest Baltimore seasons of the 1960s, '70s, and '80s. Harwell, Carneal, and Thompson called 'em so clearly, they won the Hall of Fame's Ford C. Frick Award for their brilliant baseball broadcasting.

89

Fastball Can Equal Fast Rise

Gregg Olson rose fast—from Scribner, Nebraska, to high school in Omaha to Auburn University in Alabama, then in 1988 to Baltimore. In 1989, his first full season with the Orioles, he fired his fastball right by big-league hitters. His 90 strikeouts in 85 innings, 1.69 earned run average, and 27 saves made him the American League Rookie of the Year. That award was a first for an AL reliever. In 1990 Olson's saves soared to 37. Then on July 13, 1991, in Oakland, Olson followed the trio of Bob Milacki, Mike Flanagan, and Mark Williamson to no-hit the A's in a 2-0 Baltimore victory. The four-pitcher feat had been done only once before—by those A's in 1975. Olson's other one-time moment: His only hit was a home run in 1998 with the National League's Arizona Diamondbacks. Playing so long in the designated-hitter AL, he had just four at bats his whole career.

Leave It to a Lefty to Win

Mike Cuellar's initials could have easily stood for Mr. Clutch; he was simply a high-gear pitcher. As soon as he came over in a trade with the Houston Astros after the 1968 season, the Cuban left-hander won big with Baltimore. Cuellar had award-winning production in 1969. He went 23-11 with a 2.38 earned run average to lead the O's to the first American League East title, claiming the Cy Young trophy in a tie with Detroit's Denny McLain. In the World Series, he delivered Baltimore's only victory, a 4-1 triumph in Game 1. He was even more impressive in 1970, going 24-8 and winning the Game 5 World Series clincher. Cuellar kept speeding, winning 20, 18, and 22 games while helping Baltimore to three more division titles.

That's O, as in O Hits

The Orioles wasted no time producing a no-hitter. As soon as big-league baseball lengthened the distance between the pitching mound and home plate from 50 feet to the current 60 feet 6 inches in 1893, a right-hander from Delaware named Bill Hawke grabbed his chance. Pitching at Washington on August 16, Hawke hurled a no-hitter in the Orioles' 5-0 triumph over the Senators. It was the first no-no at the new distance. Hawke finished the season 11-16. He improved to 16-9 in 1894, then left the sport after a three-year career.

Know Your No-Nos

After Bill Hawke set the tone in 1893, Baltimore pitchers produced six no-hitters over the next century. Jay Hughes polished his gem in 1898, beating Boston 8-0. The Orioles waited 60 years for another no-no. Future Hall of Famer Hoyt Wilhelm turned the trick in 1958, beating New York 1-0, the year the Yankees won it all. The O's didn't have to wait much longer. The next decade headlined three Baltimore no-hitters:

In 1967 Steve Barber and Stu Miller combined on a no-hitter at Memorial Stadium, but it was hardly a gem. The O's lost to Detroit 2-1. In 1968 Tom Phoebus beat Boston 6-0. In 1969 Jim Palmer handled Oakland 8-0. After another drought, Bob Milacki, Mike Flanagan, Mark Williamson, and Gregg Olson teamed up to choke Oakland 2-0 in 1991.

Want to Be Original? Win

Once upon a time, the Baltimore Orioles played in other leagues. These were the Orioles of the 1890s, of the American Association and National League—of John McGraw, Wee Willie Keeler, Hughie Jennings, and Ned Hanlon. Baltimore was an original AA team in 1882. Ten years later the Orioles were in the NL and won quickly. With Connecticut-born Hanlon managing, they took two years to leap from 10th place to first on the way to three straight pennants. Those 1894–96 Orioles starred Wilbert Robinson catching, Dan Brouthers at first base, Jennings at shortstop, McGraw at third, Joe Kelley in left field and Keeler in right—all eventual Hall of Famers, along with Hanlon. In 1899, the team starred a man of metal before Cal Ripken: pitcher Joe "Iron Man" McGinnity.

A Move Can Go Down

The Orioles franchise was actually born as the Milwaukee Brewers in 1901. Led by outfielder-manager Hugh Duffy, the Brewers went 48-89, bad enough for last place in the new American League. That was their cue to leave. They meandered down to St. Louis and became the Browns before opening day 1902. They made an amazing reversal, going 78-58, good for second place. But the good times died fast. The Browns made a habit of losing seasons, going as low as 43-111 in 1939—64 games off the pace. How dark did it get for the Browns? Someone played off Brown Shoe Company: "First in shoes, first in booze and last in the American League."

When a Team Loses, Sometimes It's Not Totally Lost

The St. Louis Browns boasted two winners before they turned into the Baltimore Orioles in 1954. Tops was George Sisler, one of the greatest players in history. The Ohioan amassed a .340 career average and twice hit the stratosphere—.407 with a then-record 257 hits in 1920, and .420 two years later. The first baseman landed in the Hall of Fame in 1939. Then there was Pete "One Arm" Gray. The Pennsylvanian lost his right arm in a childhood accident—and managed to make the major leagues. He played in 77 games for the 1945 Browns, hitting .218 and firing in three assists from the outfield.

Wait for a World of Difference

The Browns did win the pennant once. They clinched it while World War II raged in 1944. With loads of big-league talent in military uniforms, players in St. Louis uniforms took advantage. The Browns won the American League by one game, thanks to Nels Potter's 19-7 pitching and Vern Stephens's 20-homer, 109-RBI hitting. The Browns took their 89-65 record into the World Series, where the other St. Louis team waited. The Cardinals stood 105-49 and starred Stan Musial. Still, the Browns would have taken a 3-0 Series lead if not for an 11-inning Game 2 loss. The Cards then came back from their 2-1 Series deficit to wrap it up in six games.

Line Up Your Best Players

If you were to field an Orioles team to beat any club in history, whom would you include? Maybe these Birds:

First base: Eddie Murray
Second base: Davey Johnson
Shortstop: Cal Ripken Jr.
Third base: Brooks Robinson
Left field: Don Buford
Center field: Paul Blair
Right field: Frank Robinson

Catcher: Rick Dempsey
Designated hitter: Ken Singleton
Right-handed pitcher: Jim Palmer
Left-handed pitcher: Dave McNally
Reliever: Gregg Olson
Manager: Earl Weaver

98

Go Way Back for Greatness

What if your greatest team came from the original Baltimore Orioles and St. Louis Browns? You might suit up this bunch:

First base: George Sisler (Browns, 1915–27)
Second base: Marty McManus (Browns, 1920–26)
Shortstop: Hughie Jennings (Orioles, 1893–99)
Third base: John McGraw (Orioles, 1891–99)
Left field: Joe Kelley (Orioles, 1892–98)
Center field: Baby Doll Jacobson (Browns, 1915–26)
Right field: Wee Willie Keeler (Orioles, 1894–98)
Catcher: Wilbert Robinson (Orioles, 1890–99)
Pitcher: Urban Shocker (Browns, 1918–24)

The Farm Can Grow on You

In 1903 the big leagues abandoned Baltimore, so the city turned to minor-league ball. Enter the Orioles of the Eastern League, which turned into the International League in 1911. These Orioles left a huge mark in 1914, when Babe Ruth made a short appearance on his way to becoming the greatest player in history. The minor-league O's swept to seven straight pennants from 1919 to 1925, but they saved their best for 1944. Despite a fire that destroyed Oriole Park—near the current Oriole Park—they reached the postseason and drew big crowds to Municipal Stadium. Big-league bosses liked what they saw, and ten years later they rewarded Baltimore by moving the St. Louis Browns there. The minor-league O's relocated to Richmond and became the Virginians.

Minor Points Can
Lead to Major Standing

How good were those Jack Dunn–managed Orioles of the minors? In 2001, researchers Bill Weiss and Marshall Wright ranked the top 100 minor-league teams of all time. Three of those Baltimore clubs stood in the top 10. The best of the bunch was the 1921 outfit, ranked number 2 of all time. Those Orioles went 119-47, with first baseman Jack Bentley bashing the ball at a .412 clip. At number 5 were the 1924 Orioles, with a 117-48 record. Leading the way was future majors mound-master Lefty Grove, who went 26-6. At number 9 came the 1920 Orioles. They went 110-43, with center fielder Jake Jacobson hitting .404.

Sometimes Fans Deserve a Hand

September 6, 1995, really was one of the great nights in Baltimore history. Cal Ripken set the streak record. He high-fived fans in a lap around the Camden Yards warning track. Three years after Oriole Park opened, no wonder there was a sign that said: "The House That Cal Built." Ripken would finish with all-time Baltimore records that still stood as of 2007: 3,184 hits, 431 homers, 603 doubles, 1,647 runs, 1,695 runs batted in. And Ripken would forever connect with his biggest number: 2,632. Years after he broke Lou Gehrig's record of 2,130, he wrote in *Get in the Game*: "As I walked off the field that night, I saw somebody holding up a sign that read, *We consider ourselves the luckiest fans on the face of the earth*."

About the Author

Bucky Fox was born in New York, but plugged into plenty of Orioles action.

While growing up in the U.S. military community in Heidelberg, Germany, he caught Brooks Robinson's glove act on radio while the O's grabbed the 1970 World Series.

While at Boy Scout summer camp in 1971, Bucky tuned in his transistor to the All-Star Game, which the American League won behind homers from Baltimore's Frank Robinson and future Oriole Reggie Jackson.

While attending the University of Missouri, he saw the amazing award upset of 1973, when Baltimore's Jim Palmer outvoted strikeout record-breaker Nolan Ryan for the Cy Young.

During his days as sports editor of the *Sentinel* in Carlisle, Pennsylvania, he covered the 1979 Birds as they took a 3-1 World Series lead in Pittsburgh—before blowing it back home.

While covering sports for the U.S. military newspaper *Stars & Stripes* in Europe, he stayed close to the radio in England listening to Eddie Murray jack two homers in Game 5 as the O's closed out the 1983 World Series.

Now living in the Los Angeles area, Bucky follows the Orioles from afar and hits games at Angel and Dodger stadiums.

Beyond the ballparks, he works as a newspaper editor, runs BuckyFox.com, and writes baseball books, the first two of which were *The Mets Fan's Little Book of Wisdom* and *The Highflying Angels*.